TREASURE HUNT
IN THE
LOST CITY

Written by **Dan Abnett**
Illustrated by **Alan Baker**

a Salamander book
Published by Salamander Books Limited
LONDON

A SALAMANDER BOOK

Published by Salamander Books Ltd.,
129-137 York Way,
London N7 9LG,
United Kingdom.

© Salamander Books Ltd., 1996

Distributed by Random House value Publishing, Inc.,
40 Engelhard Avenue,
Avenel, New Jersey 07001

A CIP catalog record for this book is available from the library of Congress.

ISBN 0-517-14188-4

All correspondence concerning the content of this volume should be addressed to
Salamander Books Ltd.

1 3 5 7 9 8 6 4 2

CREDITS

Editor: Helen Stone
Colour separation by: Pixel Tech, Singapore
Printed in China

YOUR QUEST BEGINS HERE...

Robert and Anna, two intrepid treasure hunters, are planning a trip to the South American jungle where they intend to follow the path of the mysterious Mister Strange. The famous explorer left on an expedition to the legendary lost city some time ago and has not been heard of since. Over the past month, his trusty butler, Graves, has received several anonymous packages in the mail. There were no letters of explanation and no return address, but each had a South American postmark and contained a single remarkable object.

Robert and Anna have gathered the objects here to take on their journey as they believe these odd items offer clues to the whereabouts of Mister Strange and the lost treasure.

You are invited to join the treasure hunt to the lost city. If you accept the challenge, get your passport and make your way to the airport where a plane is waiting to whisk you over the Andes. From this point, you will travel through the jungle spotting further clues and solving riddles along the way. You must carve your own path through the jungle which can be a confusing wilderness to those unfamiliar with its geography. From time to time, you may find yourself back at a spot that you have already explored. If you have solved the puzzles and noted the necessary clues in this place, you should continue on your journey. The jungle is full of hidden dangers and you must be alert at all times.

Good luck, treasure hunter!

DOWNRIVER

"This is one amazing adventure," said Robert, with a smile. "I still can't believe that we're going to visit an authentic South American pyramid."

"And that there are so many extraordinary animals to see," said Anna, listing yet another species in her notebook. "Do you think we'll find Mister Strange along the way?" she asked Graves, who had agreed to accompany them as their guide.

"Mister Strange set off on his expedition some months ago and I haven't heard a word from him since. He has traveled through this country before and knows its ways, but it is filled with hidden dangers for the likes of you and me. We must proceed with caution and keep our wits about us," warned Graves, in his most serious voice. "But right now, our most pressing problem is which turn to take in the river ahead."

The river fork is not marked on our intrepid explorers' map and so you must decide which route to take. Anna has been listing the different animals that make their home in the forest. How many can you see? Score 4 points for each mammal, 3 points for each fish, 2 points for each bird, and 1 point for each reptile. If your total score is an even number, follow the river to page 8. If it is odd, take the fork with the rapids to page 18. Before you go, can you see an unusual object which suggests that Mister Strange has passed this way?

THE RAGGED GORGE

"I'm sure Mister Strange would have visited this valley," said Graves. "These rare butterflies are only found here and I know he would have wanted to study them."

"This is incredible. The climb up here was well worth the effort – I've never seen such beautiful butterflies!" said Anna with a gasp.

"Look, Graves! I can see the pyramid down in the valley. But how do we reach it?" wondered Robert.

How many butterflies can you see? Three of them have a different pattern from the rest. Can you find them? Hidden in the undergrowth, there is an object left by Mister Strange. Can you see it? If so, take the rope bridge to page 10. If not, take the tunnel on the left to page 14.

THE CITY GATES

"This must be the entrance to the lost city," said Robert, "but which doorway will lead us to the pyramid?"

"According to my book, the people who once lived here believed that animals had magical powers," said Anna, "so maybe the animals will lead the way."

"A most unscientific theory," mused Graves, "but it might just work!"

Can you find the animals that match the ones carved in the wall? If you can find three parrots, go through the lefthand door to page 12. Two snakes take you through the center doorway to page 14, and one jaguar leads through the righthand doorway to page 18. If you have found all the animals, the choice is yours! Before you leave, can you see anything that Mister Strange may have left behind him?

THE PYRAMID

"At last – the pyramid! But still no sign of Mister Strange," said Anna with a sigh.

"The people who built this ancient pyramid decorated it with hieroglyphs," explained Graves, "and it has taken many years for experts to decipher the codes. I note you had the foresight to bring along your code book, Robert."

"Yes. The codes on this side of the pyramid are number sequences. Along the bottom row, the numbers run in order on alternate panels. The first panel has one spot, the third has two spots and the seventh has four spots so, even though the fifth panel is hidden, I know it has three spots!" concluded Robert.

Robert has broken the code to the bottom row of panels. Can you work out the rules of the number sequences on the other rows and find the missing numbers hidden by the creeping vines? Anna was wrong in thinking that there is no sign of Mister Strange. Can you see something he has left hanging around? There are also two unusual objects to collect, which may come in handy later if you have to fly. To continue on your journey, take the bottom doorway to page 14, the middle doorway to page 18, or one of the doors at the top to page 16.

THE LABYRINTH

"Oh no, a giant maze!" groaned Graves, "we're sure to get lost in here!"

"Not necessarily," said Anna. "We've got a compass and we could leave a trail behind us so we know which paths we have explored already."

"Good thinking!" said Robert, "Let's go!"

Follow the maze to find the way out on the other side of the labyrinth. If you find the exit, turn to page 16. If you stop to examine an object that may have been left by Mister Strange, turn to page 12. If you notice something that you have already seen before on your journey, you may turn to page 10. If you end up back where you started, turn to page 8.

THE TEMPLE BALLPARK

"According to my book, this is the place where ancient ceremonial ball games were played," said Anna.

"This is so," agreed Graves, "The games played here symbolized the struggle between good and evil and would have had great importance."

"I guess these carvings are warriors or protective spirits then," said Robert, taking a photograph for his collection.

"This is a sacred site," said Graves, "Can you think of a better place to hide a treasure?"

Take a close look at the carved figures around the ballpark. They all look very similar, but only two are exactly the same. Can you see a clue which suggests that Mister Strange was here? Is there something he might have removed as a sign of respect at this sacred site? If you find the clue, take the staircase to page 20. If not, go to page 18.

THE MUDSLIDE

"This can't be right!" exclaimed Graves. "There is no mention of a mudslide on any of our maps!"

"Well, it looks like the only way out is to go up," said Robert, "and these vines seem strong enough to climb."

"But where do they lead and which vine do we choose?" puzzled Anna.

The mudslide is a dead end and the vines are your only hope of escape. Only one vine leads to the top of the wall. If you can find this one, turn to page 8. If not, you will become stuck in the mud and will have to wait here and hope to be rescued.

THE PYRAMID PLAZA

"Wow! This must be the very top of the pyramid! Look at all the monkeys. They appear to be quite tame," said Robert with a smile.

"They seem to be guarding those strange objects hidden in the bushes," said Anna

"Hmm... Those objects look like parts of a machine to me," said Graves, "they are not damaged in any way so they must have been hidden here on purpose."

"Remember the plan you received in the mail," said Anna, "and the necklace. I think the symbol on the necklace is a clue to the hidden treasure."

There are thirteen monkeys running wild in the plaza. Can you see them all? Do you know what the dismantled object is and how to make it whole again? Anna thinks she has found a connection between the necklace sent to Graves and the plaza. If you can see the same connection, and think that this is a path worth following, go through the doorway on the far right to page 22. If you think this connection is unlikely to be fruitful, go through the arched doorway to page 18.

THE GOLDEN GROTTO

"By Jove, there's Mister Strange!" exclaimed Graves.

"And it looks like he has something to celebrate!" said Robert.

"I'm glad my clues were of some help to you," said Mister Strange, greeting the treasure hunters. "The ancient people of the lost city built their temple around this magic spring. This spring feeds the plants which produce an everlasting food supply. This is the most valuable treasure of all. Please, come and join us for a cup of the local delicacy – cocoa."

Congratulations! You have found the treasure. However, there are some final puzzles to solve. Look carefully! Two of Mister Strange's guests are wearing identical outfits. In the grotto, there are golden statues of animals that a keen treasure hunter would have noticed on the journey. Where have you seen these animals before? You have just one last problem – how will you get home? If you don't know already, collect the red objects on pages 12, 13, 20 and 21, consult the plan sent in the mail, then take off to page 24.

Well done, treasure hunter! You have found Mister Strange and the hidden treasure. The plans for Mister Strange's plane that you brought with you have been invaluable and now you are ready to fly off into the sunset. Before you leave, retrace your steps through the jungle to see if you can spot the magical jaguar hiding and watching your every move. But first – the solutions to the puzzles:

DOWNRIVER

The hidden mammals are shown here in blue, the fish in red, the birds in yellow, and the reptiles in green. Mister Strange has left his camera on the rock next to the armadillo.

THE RAGGED GORGE

The three different butterflies are: above and to the left of Graves' head; above the central mountain; and to the left of the base of the tree. Mister Strange has left behind a pair of boots above the red flower in the bottom righthand corner.

THE CITY GATES

The three parrots are found: to the left of the parrot carving; to the right of the jaguar carving; and to the right of the righthand doorway. The two snakes are found: below the central doorway; and to the right of the righthand doorway. The jaguar is above the snake carving. Mister Strange has left behind a water bottle to the right of the righthand doorway.

THE TEMPLE

Mister Strange has left a rope running down the righthand side of the pyramid. Starting from the top row, the number sequences run as follows:
(1 3 5 7 9) – odd numbers running in order.
(1 4 5 9 14) – each number is the sum of the previous two, i.e. 1 + 4 = 5, 5 + 4 = 9 etc.
(2 1 4 3 6 5) – alternate panels have even and odd numbers running in order.
(6 1 5 2 4 3 3) – alternate panels have numbers in order, counting up or down.

THE LABYRINTH

Mister Strange has left his backpack behind.

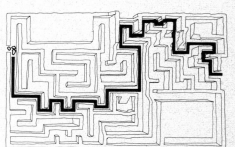

THE TEMPLE BALLPARK

The two matching carvings are in the main row, second from the left and third from the right. Mister Strange's pith helmet is above the far right carving next to the staircase.

THE MUDSLIDE

This is a wrong turn. There are no signs of Mister Strange. The only way out is to climb up the vine to Anna's left.

THE PYRAMID PLAZA

The thirteen monkeys are hidden as follows: three on the arch above Graves's head; one next to the small pillar behind; one on the central pillar and one at its base; one in the center doorway on page 20; one either side of the arched doorway on page 21; one on the carving in front of Anna; one on the pillar in front of Robert; one hiding behind the pillar directly in front; one in the bottom righthand corner. Anna has spotted the symbol for "chocolate" above the doorway next to her that matches the necklace sent to Graves. Mister Strange's plane has been dismantled and is hidden in the bushes.

THE GOLDEN GROTTO

The woman in the bottom righthand corner and the woman sitting behind the table of fruit are wearing identical outfits. The golden statues match some of the animals which Anna noted in her book as the group traveled downriver on pages 6 and 7.